Black Girl Mango Seeds

Melissa Jones

Acknowledgements

I would like to first give thanks to my friends and family for supporting me and believing in my vision. Special shout out to guitarist John Givens for creating the book cover. I want to thank the lovely Tyanna Davis for being a part of my vision. She is the beautiful face of Black Girl Mango Seeds! I want to thank Schlisha Lakia Davis-Hollie for capturing such a wonderful photo.

I want to give thanks to all of those beautiful women who agreed to have their photos featured in the book:
Joy Elan, Shani B, Lady Diva, Ayanna Robinson, Paige Mayes, Marilyn Miner, Dom Jones, Joymara Coleman, Sabrina Cupid, Mia, Inayah Baaqee, Ifafunke Olagabaju, Erica Jackson, Daisy Ozim, Mayah Dawson, Cristen Spencer, Ariana Jackson, Hadiyah Owens, Kanisha Pretty Black, Safiya Leslie, Georgette Mayers, Dalaun, Kelitah Kalonda, Lisa Oduor Noah and photographer Yuwei Huang, Ashley Wilkerson and photographer Daryl Jim, Susan Yen and photographer David West and designer Tonya Nichols, Anne-Florence Pungong, Olivia Musoke, and Christina Mason.

I want to acknowledge Lola's African Apparel and Renee's Bakery for providing services and support during the book release. I want to also thank Marcus Newsome for the wonderful artistic designs for the Black Girl Mango Seeds shirts.

I would like to thank Tyson Amir for helping me through the publishing process as well as offering extra feedback. I would like to acknowledge Casey Dawes for her knowledge and expertise on publishing resources.

Throughout this process, I want to thank my dear and closest friends for listening to my ideas and for just being amazing throughout my creative process, my growth, and my overall development as a person. Thank you Tracy Cruz for being an amazing and endearing friend. Thank you Muziki Wa Ulimwengu for the encouragement and support. Thank you Ifafunke Olagabaju once again for being trustworthy and compassionate. I appreciate you. I want to thank my bandmates No Lovely Thing for being awesome. Music is truly healing and wonderful. From the poems and songs I have written, it has helped me grow tremendously. So thank you to Sarah Iyer, Yunoka Berry, John Givens, Jae Jackson, Milos Nikic, and JonAnthony Floyed-Jackson. I also want to thank Kevin Goldberg for wanting to collaborate and write new music with me. Music and writing is a huge part of me and I thank everyone that has played a huge role in my creative process. Thank You Audacious Iam for hosting writing sessions at your place. It helped me to maintain focus and it provided a space for me to share and gain really good feedback.

Thank you Mom (Patsy Bize) for being the beautiful woman you are, through pain and through triumphs. I love you.

Introduction

Why Black Girls?
Because this is about them.
It is designed for them to be heard, recognized throughout moments in time.
Because they matter.
Because they are magic.
Always.

Why Mango?
Because it is the sweetest fruit.
Because it derives from hot/tropical places.
Because it represents fruitfulness and brightness.
Because Black girls are bright.
Sweet
Fruitful
Because their melanin is everything
And the sun loves them.

Why seeds?
Because it is implanting knowledge.
Because this book represents planting stories for people to see Black girls.
Really see them.
Because seeds represent growth, nature, soul, roots, and the beginning of time.
Because seeds represent issues that have plagued Black girls
Because seeds represent magic that happens and that continues to happen.
The purpose is to continue sharing important stories.
To name experiences.
To be human.
To be empowered.   To be change.

"You cannot police me so get off my areolas" -Janelle Monae

1. You are a loveshack
waiting to be rocked with purple trees
lining window panes.
I know you think
I am ordinary,
weak even.
Bubble gum wrappers in my purse.
Middle finger spray in my left jean pocket.
Go on ahead.

2. We are different. I'd like my lips to be Marilyn Monroe red and
my hair rude
like Monday night fights,
Mayweather fists with a tint of lavender embroidery.

3. I'm not some toy with fantastical emotions here.
Now I'd like to feel naked today por favor.
Not for the attention.
It's just that my valleys below are centered
with clusters of peppermint cinnamon streams.
They need original sunlight.

4. You want a tiny shadow by me.
No flavor in the depths of my uterus.
You say my ambition is vulgar,
impulsive
and
offensive even.
oh it's time for my middle finger spray.

5. Left pocket.
Yes.

Jeans with the holes in them,
where you try to put all of your rusty fingers in,
mind-control me with that professor charm.
My hand-mirror wants to smack you,
reflect your foolery.
I'd like to explore more of myself.
My sweets and my innocence.
My spicy and my wilds.
wilds. colors. 5 4 3 2 uno.

Excerpt:

This is for Black women who want to reclaim their body.
use it.
no standards.
no expectations.
no excuses.
free the body.
free the nipple.
free the impulse
reclaim.
Replenish.

Formation (Come on now ladies let's get in formation)

Angela Davis: oppressed at this special time   political
vibrations   statements   attention attention attention
awaits

revolutionary
overturn

Audre Lorde: simply because unicorns rummage the earth with its
might
the colors
brown painted ladies
in fallopian tendril skies
those ladies dance because they can   they can   affirm their
secret jellies

Fannie Lou Hamer: up my dress and down my dress   the
covering of my head

the silencing of my body   the voice in the cell   screaming and
high pitched laughter

on my face

death wishes

and Mississippi drownings

patrolman   decent lives   just want to live   just want to
register just…..*cut to the President*

Ella Baker: Just the backbone   the spine   to advocate
organize to be free   trying

to take those chains off   so tight   those marks

the simple roll of the mind

such power
encouragement
look to yourself to emerge   those marks
flickering off in the wind

Black Girl #1 Desireé

Legs purring

    Louisiana
Mississippi
Alabama

    in a vase bowl

Cellulite twerking
conceptualizing country daffodils

    She: the items.   The fine tooth comb. The romper.   She
gave birth to creole herds and second helpings

We be dancin' like fools in dirty water
I'd stay on those rivers
till I wrinkle hot pepper

    She
The tide
The flava'
The beehive
on her chariot

That vase bowl
    Sun down
and the light still bathing in those valleys

Commentators' Transcript

Serena Williams vs. Maria Sharapova

Serena

_____

_____

-Tennis is a lot more colorful now with the Williams' sisters
- She looks a bit dizzy out there. As almost as if she has taken something.
-Natural athleticism with a powerful body
-She definitely was not thinking about the placement of that shot
-Serena does not look happy about that
-Yes, Jimmy Connors used to get so angry
but for Serena that is unacceptable behavior
-She should calm down a bit before getting fined
-She has a muscular frame
-Her rivals try not to emulate her physique
-She is a BEAST out there
Manly   gorilla   savage

<drop shot>

"don't even look at me I am not the one"-Serena Williams
<<<<<<< **Tennis Net**

Maria

-Russian beauty

-Testing positive for banned substance

-Lenient slap on the wrist

-She knows how to spin and put things in her favor

-There seems to be a different rule for her

-Maria Sharapova has some of her best photoshoots as a model

-Forbes highest paid female athlete

-We were hoping she would have retired to become a lingerie model by now

-She loses endorsement deals with nike

-Her career will only be lost for six weeks

-lesson learned and facing consequences

-lenient slap on the wrist   beautiful   slim goddess   double ace

Undocumented Story

I saw a man

      with a black bird

 its wing stretched   pointed straight   claws bent back   chirping
muted

His forehead frowned

      ocean waves

I was 4

and he

pulled the

big black bird

made it sound

like a jet plane

My mother screamed

It did not sound like those times she sang good morning to me

It sounded like the black bird grew into a demon

like a jet plane crashing against everything

It sounded like….

I remember being taken in by this woman

For only a few days

she had a little girl

                        who smiled with oreos in her mouth

when she tongue kissed me

with her vanilla tongue

I thought she was

             a mama bird

pushing her tongue into my mouth

like a sea of rocks

touching me in my no-no spot

I ran to the bathroom

used someone else's toothbrush

used someone else's towel

used someone else's pain

opened my eyes

into a new home

with stuffed animals on the floor

They were my audience

but

could they protect me?

could they fight off black birds?

could they fight and protect black girls from

black tongues and white swirls?

could they save me?

Black girl #2 June

JUST gonna walk outside with no bra on today   but I may get
stopped by Jesus

And his crew

Sometimes my mind is airy
like a fresh sheet hanging in the backyard
floating in the wind
beneath the sunlight
and I'd see my 12 year old self

Certainly small

with large breasts

Their eyes diverting toward my chest

 an ice cream stain

and

    knickerbockers

the days where my mother and father were many people

"We have left you in the system poor girl"
Their eyes were watching a child

Their eyes were watching fear

Their eyes were watching GOD SHIPS pointing missiles with elasticity

I've grown to not apologize for these berries

Or breasts

Playtime trails off into wonder

into brothers that don't care

into sisters that shame and criticize

Just gonna walk outside naked

 in wingspan pose

 in sight

to exist even when they don't

Want

Me   To

Dear Black woman

You are beautiful
You are valued
You are important

    I still believe that mountains are capable of being
moved
    that jungles can operate successfully with your musk
mixed with moon

that art can be
    the way you walk

the way light bounces off of your furrowed brows

    and I know that emotion
in which you are allowed to feel

    You are extraordinary either way

From
another Black woman

Two brown girls kissing

Aloe you.   Wild potted thick   Smelling of sage
        On these victorian steps

We grew up on strips of wonder and pomegranate

    The cement spilling over meditated swans

We swapped purple secrets

        about thighs heavier in the nights

about guava secretions
                    Tattoo on your clit
I created
miracles with
   my sorcerous lizardry
Flicking tongues on
        savored drops of Nairobi

            You bent over to retrieve your maple

We're on shrine
in bantu knots
oily sweat and
black soap

You
pink lemonade
tangy salamander

I slip my tongue on life
melanin   dragon fruit   and destiny

Moral of this story, leave the black women in the ghetto. Get you a white girl."-Terrence Howard

black women in leaves

morals in black

morals in white

stories in you

girl, you a story in black

this story leaves you

you get ghetto

you get white leaves of this story

you leave women in black

black in women

you   leave

Get you a black story

This white girl   leaves (leaves) in black women

ghetto story

white in the black of moral

Missing Black Girl

(Washington, DC)

Name: Bayou
Oshun
and helicopter tongue

Height: mini pyramid of Khafre

Weight: she carry burden   she
the tons of blood   and
elephant's' tears
overalls and paint brushes   left to cover
moles and
        jaundice thoughts

Dob: Summer time orange
year 1990. Weather of the iris. Moments like this
brown baby developed into a
                  map of transatlantic flower petals
As young as
skipping feet
chewing gum leaves
toes in the color of shasta punch
takis and memes
dancing shea buttery thighs

Eyes: maple
The last corner of the waffle square
The in between stages filled of full and moderate
Spongy-like sometimes
depending on the circumstances

They droop
and swelter
and breathe in
and soak in sweets and batter

Hair: Winter and the creaky branches on the mountain tops
The way the vines coil up
The nature's way of intentionality
patterns of interwoven nests
Red-throated loons in between follicles

Last SEEN:

The corner of North and South. Fumbling with hands. Wearing
black body.
Interchangeable visibility
Possibly with known assailant
White   noise

Breaking News: Police are searching for a 15-year-old Caucasian
Hamilton girl who went missing on Tuesday.

More pressing more pressing more pressing more pressing more
more more more

Michelle

Monkey face SHE-man Monday
They thought they could name a day
and place their lips on a frying pan
name a day
 but couldn't separate distance between a woman and a
_____/

A line slash

Those thoughts
ENOUGH.

Because she was my Wife Crush Monday-Sunday

AND

I've heard the hummingbirds sing tunes like "Oh happy day"
I've heard Eartha Kitt purr instantly
with insatiable thirst
with pretty brown brown against yellow

Michelle
The skin
The Queen
The flotus
The grace
I remember an image of you not smiling
I remember an image of you in red
And all of things said about how you're supposed to be

There are plenty of line dashes with ill intent

_____/

black/woman/magic/always/wins

When words are put together and faces are collaged into one big
Jameela Ashley Monica Keisha Alexis

That is the pot of Michelle
Of all the things I've wanted since talking
Girl from the south side

Honey   Chai   filter

 Journeys of futures
Malia
Sasha
Black and white photos
Of matching outfits
And we wonder where time has gone

When you've danced and pearls became apart of your voice
And we've been raised in your kitchen

Euclid Ave
black keys
A tune with an acquired taste

We can say hey girl hey
to you
Sing lyrics with southern grooves

Everyday

No such thing as farewell
We've watched several of us emerge
Popping out of gardens of hope   introduced to orchards and piano
benches
And I sit
just like the ones who look like you
learning those same tunes

Black woman # 3 Grace

I read many books to the girls   they looked at me and pointed
that my glasses were magic

The violet tint   the way my eyes danced around   as they
commented on the various teachings of literature

all the while

channeling Gwendolyn Brooks

Jazz junes

Cool blues

Think straight

Brown capes

When we walk to the nearest seat

The desk with all of those books

I have them choose
they know
Brooks and Angelou
Ms. Grace

I'll listen
For girls to gather around to share their stories

To speak loud but firm

When can we make it a holiday to speak with such conviction?

I study

We study

I go home

lavish my skin

Reflect on the essence

of my reflections

Prepare

with violet tints   real cool

 real cool

Lemon Tree

Backyard patio

Yellow trimmings

of my panty line

We played hookie

told you I was experienced

that I colored the bricks with skin and ends of butterfly wings

They come

like sun down

An evolution of ice cream stained overalls

Lemons

we sweated from our arms

You laughed when I came home

I rolled over to see the trees stagnant

Hot sun

Juice

The cracks and paraded grass

My braids around your torso

You've invested time in   poetic justice

Comment about Lupita Nyong'o

"Everybody saying her skin looks beautiful, how about her face though…" -G.A.

Mombasa sand

      stuck to tongue
      stuck to misfortune
      stuck to his reflection

      Now I've met a girl with Nyong'o skin

She held my hand
as the wind shouted with bones in its throat
Mombasa sand
down the legs of Africa

      She still glistened
told me her dark berries were delicate
made me sign my name on her ancestors' breaths

      When we whisper

we leave out parts   we trail on the Nile with just our eyes
      but when we project our voices

the birds marry our octaves
carry our wounds
swallow the fluid from our faces

Her face

like Lupita
like Khoudia Diop
like God
like pomegranate loving on full lips
like bright swahili tones and calming nights
like chamomile and fluttering tea steeped in cups
like migrations through Serengeti

Yet his face

like most sunken places
like the sounds of horrid squawking of
vultures feasting

Lest we not forget

that there is no comparison

Her shit better

Black.
when you spend your time comparing the color of your high
cheekbones with your bowels

My light skin friend Katherine,

she'd tongue twist my hair and barbecue my slave name
Williams-Jones-Smith-Weston-Harris- Johnson
I'd forget which one I gave myself to

She'd smell my pussy
tell me hoodlums were filling me up with twinkies and
over-processed ejaculatory cancer
saying I deserved to be   Raggedy Ann well
Raggedy Anita   cuz I was forest dark

the moon   wrapped around her throat when she spoke
talkin' about shining light on me

talkin' about I'm a dark wolf   different breed

She,

Red bone

That light skin voodoo shit

She'd pray and pour her speckled colored feces on me   and a
hum and a woo and a hum and a woo
Her shit better

 I'd go on and cry until

I'd make her proud by
dipping my face in powdered beignets

Walk around
let boys rummage through my temple just to feel obese

They'd love me eventually
with all me
out in the open

Black.
Forest dark   howling

oh Raggedy Anita   everyone wants a Raggedy Anita

bullshit.

Trying to be

Stained on your face towel
can I borrow a face?
remember the inkwell
with the piss drawn smiles?

You told me I had to be a pink argonaut
do it like this
don't ever shit in the toilet
spill your glitters and mix

I barely recognized humanness
woman-less
give it back, my pussy,
you pussy.
arghhh
I walked around frustrated
with a poorly drawn sketch of a dick
broken in fours

I was trying to do some spell and shit
my web coiled arms splitting
this is what I was told to be
back in the ocean I go

Girlfriend for a day

I kissed her ripples on tongue

           the spit upon her chin

translucent

we traded mermaid fins

saliva dreams

and momma-poppa

dialogue of 'honey

gimme a kiss before

you leave'

The sun canvassed

blotches on her cheeks

she laughed

smelled my desperation

my fear

my panting

the ice-cream truck

saved us

hit us with an interlude

of do your ears hang low

and does my hair

have all of the

beads connected to

the ends

My mom would question

how they fell off

and

I would say I was running

From Jesus

Toward him

Maybe

If she'd kiss me like that again

I would like it better the next time

Like it if she'd play a good daddy

to my black baby dolls

give me pretend money

to pretend to go shopping with

my pretend adult friends

like Gina Payne and

Khadijah James

the way she wore her

overalls

one strap up

the other strap

down

Does this mean we're gay?   she asked me.

Don't say a thing

Don't tell them

We connected tongues

and stuffed our bras

with dark sun

Don't tell them

My hip still

attached to an

overall strap

swan between legs

swimming in a secret pond

and I just wanted to play house

with a pretend boy

Just wanted to be

I was daddy's boy
but my overalls were showing my figure

I fought a girl and a boy outside my house
I remember her shoe flying at me
my soul bursting through her face

I wrestled the boy and kicked him in his privates
I didn't wanna be a boy
but I wanted to be tough like Daddy
tough like
yelling at my Mom tough
tough like
frowning at everybody tough
tough like
I'm gonna beat yo ass tough

My house was broken into again
My Kenya doll was stolen from a "friend"
My sister yelled at me for wearing her clothes
My momma said I would be big as a house one day
My daddy said I need to get over my nightmares

but my overalls were showing my figure
I could tell my walks to the corner store
were like walks through television sets

me
just where have my itty bitty titities gone
I just wanted to be tough like daddy
I wasn't ready
to be me

Black girl # 4 Gia

She pulled my hair

I was 13

      scrambling through

flies
    and

      mustard earth

to find curly strands

    deep raisin color

      under fire

* you think you cute or somethin'*
* all of you light skinned girls*
I only wanna talk to your bones
I only like red tints underneath it all
and you can be a poster on my wall
* You ain't really black*

Scrambling through

    a cluster of bodies

shaped like judgement

    days

where you have to prove yourself

    everyday
Skin against

    coffee beans

residue

alliance to fit in and out of

mugs

    Seen and unseen

           and

hair

      strands

on

everybody's hands

Oh Nina

We found the lightest of light brights to play you in this movie

black face

She so pretty

she played Columbian once

I thought I heard wrong

you're not here

and if your spirit was visual

it would be you and your purist glowly chocolate form

with the right markings and curves upon your lips

the strange fruit that would sit right under your nose

the voice that would swallow the earth whole

cleanse the waxy minds

protest in song

spells

enchantment

That Blackness

That Black Power

That

That

beauty

we have a culture

yes?

We need you Nina

You say when you're needed

you have to give

yes?

That Blackness

That

That

Black Power

but oh Nina

That girl playing black face

you

see

that?

Hollywood

I crack a smile

with disgust

and listen to revolutionary songs

That Blackness

sangin'

Nina Simone

                            bring me your soul   just a little bit closer
content   meaning and hymns

we need you:

"To me we are the most beautiful creatures in the whole
world...Black people. I mean that in every sense."

-Nina Simone

Do I move you?

yes.

She attempts to portray you but I am unmoved by that.

darker fruit

Dripping pigment and blood leaves

a strange dynamic

behind the camera the director yells "cut"

fix your nose

fix the blend of highlighted textures

how can we authenticate the real you Nina?

Through music:
Oh Baltimore

Man it's hard to live

just live

You know our babies are dying

you know

we sing the blues with you

whenever we need you

we play our stereos

no need to recreate

a bloomed flower

Oh Nina

it's hard to recreate your story

we let your songs play

through speakers

relevant

occurrences

belted

in the most revolutionary way

Facebook Status from V.R. "Most black women aren't loyal or faithful...fact they keep a side nigga or two...just in case nigga fuck up...options like a auction they come and go..."

Just in case something happens with Tyrell
there is always a Sam
there is always a Pedro
there is always a Mr. Postman
bringing dreams and headaches

I sat and listened to the radio with shadows climbing onto my lips
like painted outlines of bears
My words only whispers through forests
My bedtime song
My own voice
My own heart

Just in case something happens to You
I'll be rubbing aloe vera
and butter
on my senses
I'll be
with my other sisters
shaving
the flakes
from your ooze drops
and bad habits
I'll be penetrating
myself with my own
light
fingers
after a movie
about dance
Glory

and
Fro's
like Donna Summers

To the side I keep string   gauze   tulips   and tweezers
The smell of you like a freight train
gnawing at my waist
You bite marked beads   I clipped with scissors
that's at my side
restitching waist with tulips   marigolds   and edges from sun

My side rib
My side edge liquid honey
My sidearm

My options
like Maldives and capers
waters and fruitful

If you have yet to understand
you'll live not knowing
why that woman left you
brown and freckled
skipping out
hot with music
and eyebrows curious for the world
She eats better
She breathes and climaxes ten times
She gives no fucks
At her side
whilst a thorn
and release

Black is beautiful shawty

Wale said that
after
lotus
flower
bomb

You know when he can overlook my damaged edges
and cram his sentences into a sealed tight zip up bag
babyyoutheAFRICANQUEENandIlovedat

When I was nine
my hair fell out because the perm was left into long

When I was fifteen, some boy said I had a "ghetto booty"

When I was about to cut myself
after a year in a half spent with a man who told me
I was nothing without out him

I thought about the skin underneath

wondering if little hidden figures would come out and throw my
soul into some wilderness

Give me flesh that looked like fresh golden rules

"Golden touch"

After a while of fingering the corner of the adobe brick inner
workings of my spirit

I had a myriad of thoughts

like the travel time of the sweat between my breasts

or the beads of straight naps that coil and shoot back growls toward
others

It amounts to something similar
A thank you   when he can jam pack a flower with a hummingbird
on a tree protecting its' nest

near the skies of painted dancing sleep.

I used to dream of you

kissing the back of my hand like a stale contender

but I appreciate the effort

WE CAME along way from just being "slight work."

I saw your son and son's mother in the coffee shop this afternoon

Family you couldn't have

She told me he was 3

I knew that

I knew those eyes

Your eyes
Depths of deep rooted triumphs

You said maybe if she found someone   she would be good

and maybe if I found someone   I would feel love for the first time

I saw the way her hand dangled
her mouth purring few words

Her grey sweatpants hugging her
like lovers who travel and spend quality time

but
she walked with   your son   with unexplained rhythm   upright
bass down her back

Mama

Son

     You

absent from the space   a space

     Where you have no capacity to love someone new
and you think you do
Scarred

     and every Black woman

mumbles for a second

"I don't know what I am doing wrong."

     I rub my hair strands together to create a spark to disappear

Just like that

she walks away

So do I

I think you do too

Black girl #5 Melody

He told her how "rare" she was

watched the sun make love to her shoulders

                tasted the stars from her musk

different

    he said
                with intention

"Put your dominant foot forward"

Her grin swamped with pixelated eyes

   a show

a movie for the records

He'd climb on her chest

pound a slow neo soul tune

dent the hums of her name

swallow honey

she

a tent to house ideas and endless thoughts

She

a rare mural

on his tongue
wearing her

melatonin

with summer

    a sweet monolithic sound   she wanted to sing until the
evening

He said yes and then no

too embellishing for his ears   oh melody   oh too
rare   to hold

Changing

The rocks against my face are collecting soldier molecules
the pinkness and the rawness of skin exposed to hundreds of men

The desire to be with Blackness

Oceanic views somewhere in the Hamptons
a woman contemplates about her
life

like
little strings
from a violin being plucked
by rib cages belonging to La Amistad

and I
search for different skins
to borrow from kin
to borrow excess from Sarah Baartman
to borrow from men
an armor
a toughness from his
calluses
being
spilled over
egg whites

running away from
changes

Yet
another woman
opens her stomach to show the wings of
butterflies
DNA
the regions
of poisonous
African Monarchs

I get butterflies
in my stomach and throat
exposed and
pressured to be
an impenetrable fortress

my eyes
the same color as her darkened mole

I am
ironing out the rocks writing buildings on my cheeks
stamped to become a city with moderate crime seeping through
lips

Another woman passes me
her fist clenched and
a smoking gun inside her grin
tired she is
she is
I am
her
and everything
but
becoming something
ambiguous

next to different
shades of skin
changing

Forgotten One

I forgot how to spell my name after I was raped
I forgot that the bible existed
and that birds bark when they are terrified of ghosts
Maybe that's all in my head

This old mattress laid two eggs
One was the splitting of veins in an undefeatable neck
The other was the throbbing of an angelic tomb way down there
Bloody panties
dem boys don't care
my hair
nappy
dem boys don't care
Darker berries
dem boys don't care
Body wrapped in dandelion semen
Dem boys
rummaged through the island
stole the empress
filtered her with cotton
stroked her hips with iron

Iron
Cotton
Liquid

I forgot how to sing after I was raped
swinging on dead placenta from my youth
Swing low
sweet chariot

My mother would calmly close the door
to hide from my wailing
She was blacker than the coal underneath my eyes
She was hearty and meaty with a thick bottom
I'd have to pinch all over to scale off this skin to become less
recognizable
but it only drew them in
Dem boys
smelled my youth
filtered the world with their eager bodies
A mix of oily sea and chocolate snot
landed on my face
It was detrimental
to face the world with half a brain and seaweed undergarments

I'd gag on it
until I was nauseous
but then I'd remember something
The name that was taken from me
was built on a plantation
I'd remember the body my mother passed down to me
I'd remember why my holes were lynched and burned   why
the baby was dropped on its head early on

Once
I dreamt my body turned to snow white
I'd hear the birds bark on my shoulders
My mother would leave the door open
and dem boys would be tied to a pole out front

But I'd wake up with a pencil and a bloody uterus
spelling words that they'd give me
so far from my name

For Sasha (The Walking Dead)

Donny Hathaway   and the quivering of your lips

        kisses you baby
                        and all the freedom of death

when dirt is filled with your mouth

Cried brown
Cried sanctified wounds
and

inside a coffin built for you   your tongue   your rotten fragility

as you reassure the stench of suicide

You'd like to look Hathaway in the eyes

press your sweat into his words

believe your eyes to be momentous and less basic than before

        You've witnessed flesh like no other

the birth of reconstructed limbs and it's task to dismember

You sit and remember

your past lover

and the others

"Someday we'll all be free…"

    Your way
the pill
the weight and white of eyes

the screams of the saviors

    as you tear the skin with your nails and grip the necks with your teeth

It's a sensation you can't feel

    You've turned for good

You've gone to meet Donny

    and sing with him in 1973

"Someday we'll all be free…"

Black girl #6 Mistaken Identity (Justice for Kamala Harris)

It's not 1963

      You ride your bicycle so freely

Hair braided like
Iverson
and so then we
          place blame on dogs for sniffing monoliths

and basketball shorts   and black sculpted adolescent musk

      When you wanna take a sip of water

you take a sip of k9 fur sweat

You

5'2

19

mistaken for a man

You

clearly a woman

with black melted skin

wrapped around teeth

It's not 1963

Yet we still can't be
Yet we still can't breathe

Smile

Smile, woman.

It's morning time and you must have woken up next to a blood sucker

crept up on you

pout lips and

the switch

of your eyebrows to

grey forest hills

Grey.

Woman.

Igbo.

Tribal.

Honeysuckle.

Misdirected fro.

Smile, because that would make our eyes firmer

our hands warmer

our mouths to call you beauty queen

and
daylight comin' and mi waan' gooooo home

to that

to that right there

Shine yo grill

IF YOU WEREN'T SO DAMN UPTIGHT WOMAN

Can't I be pleased today?

*She walks with tight lips: SHE.....lost her dignity in the rage of
blood suckers, blue devils, mongrels, and flockers   did she like it
did she like it   ?

"Why is this man asking me to smile? I've had enough of this
day." -Says, some pouty lipped brown woman.

I am Sandra Bland

Sandy Speaks:

"Kings and Queens"

"You are beautiful"

"They should legalize being Black in America"

*Meanwhile
there's a pussy ass cop
with a pussy ass attitude
and he feels all big and bad now*

*concrete
no water
no avail
like happy season and
trigger fingers up summer dresses
and that fine ebony girl
with the crooked mouth and wide tunnel nose
He'd go deep sea diving with his short strut
His dick so far up his butt now so far now so far now*

Sandy Speaks:

"We have to establish our Queendom and Kingdom"

"Black lives matter"

*If she wasn't mentally unstable, she would be alive today

One man said after watching Sandy Speak
This is just the talk of a typical nigger playing the victim
Says
another

I am her
Because I matter
Maybe not to *them*
AND I COULD NEVER TAKE MY OWN LIFE

I'd wash my hair in shea butter   wrap my golden lips around the
goddesses of melanated skin   drink thee   enlighten brothas and
sistas   speak truths   like Badu   and twist hair in the shade where
Texas police can't find me   but they seem to find a way   into
our spaces

"Black Lives Matter"

*light your ass up   I'm hurting   an ego   a tall as negro woman
talking shit   I'll show her*

"Black Lives Matter"

*You know they killed her   and a bit of me too   She was gonna
bring down that police department   hell   the
whole county

*Can't give that little nigger too much power now
 shut her up and put her in the back*

Teary eyed Mothers

"I cannot imagine the call when you know you've outlived your child." –Wanda Johnson

No. you. Do. Not. Want. To. See. Him.
HE DOES NOT HAVE AN ESOPHAGUS

The moment his eyes looked up at me   3 weeks old   his
melanin was spreading   especially in his cheeks   he gurgled
and hiccupped dreams   he said he'll be precious   be bold be

"Their intent was to kill him"

That's right   they called them wendigos in blue   everywhere
loitering near "We sell liquor signs" and streets laced with brown
pigment and   uneven cement   skin tissues   latching onto
gated fences and mother's breasts   but

He left behind 5 boys

Face. Against.   Concrete.   Parking lot.   Cigarette butt.
Discarded chicken nugget.   Car wash receipt.   Blood.

I remember when he would wrestle with us in the backyard. His
laugh would send my other brother to the moon and back to the
floor. I think It was the pitch. Like bats trying to fight off their
predators type of laugh.

When we take our kids to the park
We watch them laugh and play
They fall and get back up
Or stay there and cry
Waiting for your arms

Your voice
Your presence
Your
"It's probably fake"
Boy brown   drum line   those drums beating   like shells to
torsos drum line
He was supposed to be   marching   behind the   glockenspiel
Toy gun
12
She could barely speak of him   we love you Tamir baby

"He was my first born but he was still my baby"- Gwen Carr
(mother of Eric Garner)

He said, "ok Momma what do you want me to bring to the
reunion?"
I said, "we'll discuss it when you get here"
He told me he loved me
That was our last conversation
"Be the voice of your child no matter what others say" –Wanda
Johnson (mother of Oscar Grant)

Black girl # 7 Mother of Irie (single black mother)

Covered in sick

              I let you pacify your dolls in scraped knees

Color
my
eyes
with shimmery shadows of legs

    We ate swarms of my wails for breakfast

I'm sorry
I left the stove in your reach
I
crammed my head in your father's coke

          When we watched our popsicle juice drop down our
thighs on the porch

I cried
You girls just
swam in sticky innocence
      watched the trail of ants live around your ankles

    I'm sorry
I yelled often

    I couldn't keep the lights on in my
brain
home

pockets
heart
      Forgive me

I try to   myself

Payton

A lawsuit

   over naps and brown patches

over whether to sing the national anthem at games

over whether you'll be called Queen

Sis

Hoodrat

over your innocent smile

but hey black child

hey

the suffering and pain you put your parents through

they'll be judged by your braided hair

your almond shaped eyes

your father's sperm

you ever being born

not of "standard" or the "purest" form

Mom,

I'd like you to wait until the black doll is available on the shelf
Oh, I see
but she doesn't have a car like the other dolls
Does that mean I won't have a car?
Am I not allowed to swim in this space freely?
With my curls playing trombone and harp along my back?
and my full lips blowing bubbles at parties
where other kids disperse like an evacuation?
Am I flame?
A volcano?
A hidden electrical wire?
You tuck me in extra tight
and read me "my black is beautiful."
Is that true?

Yesterday, I picked my daughter up from school
She said, "momma the teacher said my hair smelled bad"

Nights
long nights
the couch pillows on floor
her head against my knees
coconut oil
finger tips
eyes rolled
head turned

Her

wanting to keep her head straight
to watch her program

and

food sits on stove
Incense trails off whispers
Chandeliers dangle on second floor
Sex noises on first
Loretta kicking Johnny out on third

Fourth floor

Swift stories and
I spent my time in
 shea moisture Jamaican Black
castor oil
coconut
lime

detangler

As I wrap my fingers in curls that spell out whirl winds and high
living
I sweat off bath water
filled with silencers and hunting knives
Out to get this little one
chocolate girl
with
magic and multi-colored hair-ties

Fresh scalp
and
  her voice trailing off into cries
"The smell distracting to classmates" -Teacher

The battle between leeches and black girls

I've come too close to shoving it up that woman's nose
to thinking that her face can graze these couch pillows

And you have no fucking idea
who we are

Crowns are presented on these couch cushions
Magic is created with each braid
    Fragrance and pure greatness

and then her wailing voice tells me that my hands are like Golden
Gods

              What do we do with those that
disobey the Golden Gods? I asked her.

Off with their heads? Her response.

Well, yes sort of.

Well sometimes sweetie, people choose to ignore the Golden Gods even when it's right in front of them.
They see their worth and they become terrified of that power.

She gets it
She wipes her tears
and turns her head willingly so that I could part these last few braids

What else

What else

                    are you supposed to

use your body for?

 They walk up to me with cradled arms

                    slurpy sounds   empty plates   expecting corn
bread and embryos to play in
                  the parking lot   waiting for groceries and leggo
island   where the water is hot and the blocks are limiting   but
briefcases are full

grab her by the pussy and make it hurt

They say

my eyes are as big as my dreams   and

babies are fed to my groin through dialogue

They told me

I wasn't a woman

They say

all we do is pop them out

feed them hormonal birds
and collect checks

but me
For once I'd like to use my body to dance on an island

cry the waters

drink away labor

plunge my fist into my abdomen

take those ears and rest them underneath my armpits

burn sweat

burn- sweat the stigma, the bloody uterus and encase it in sage

Where art thou angry body?

working body

barely passing the brown paper bag test, the real hair test, the
physically fit test

But

what I use this thang for

interrogated

I'd make sure

they get a whiff of

sage in panties

before I dip into water

with my hips stationed
                              on top of my back
coasting the bloody stains

Black girl # 8 Iesha

Some days we feel alone, emotional, frustrated, overwhelmed,
confused, hurt, in pain, in sorrow, hopeless,
Down,
Down,
Down,

    I know

we have to put on a straight face
Pretend our bra straps are tangled free
Pretend
that our smile
reaches our eyes
the sun
and moon
The white collar folks
Our babies
Our babies that don't yet exist
Our lovers
Our lovers we wish we had
                but don't
and yet we still feel like we have to pretend with them so
what's the point of a "lover"

    When we cry

we get a pat on the shoulder
A cookie
A "you got this"
A "you're a strong Black woman"

A "you'll be back on your feet in no time"
A "you are used to making grave sacrifices"

        But when we cry
tears turn into golden stars

    and glitter

celebrated

for how well we've "handled"

blood from our universe
whips on our lips
cuts on our scalps
burns on our strength

    (some days)

(days)

    We feel like we have to normalize our non human
beast
nature

Turn it into stone
with purple stretch marks
Lick the dust under our breasts
Call it living this life
that some know nothing about
Only WE

Blue nail polish

When the sun
                        hits it right

Thong sandals
Blood
on the soles
from shaving
legs
        like
removing
slippery hands
up skirts

My
        favorite color is blue too (he said)
I can see your toes from a mile away
                        royal blue on chocolate

When the sun
                hits it right
blue
smudge
        like
BB King's
lips
adjusting
to the wavering
shades of brown

(he said) My toes
a reminder of the blueberry pop tart he had one morning

They (my toes) should be on the Downtown City
Blues album cover
(he said) My face dark but my toes….
My toes blue
My face blue purple
So when the sun
hits it
It really hits it
But my toes
everyone will rush to look down (he said)
Every
One

Diary of expectations

Lips
                    the color of premature birth
where
the weather is
plum red labor

I must want you
I must want every other man
I must want a date
in the back of someone's Honda

                                because my eyes said
"fuck me"
I decided
 I didn't want to cross my legs

Thighs needing to breathe sultry satellites from stars
Those beggars wanting
Those liars talking
about how I want "it"

How my butt seemingly protrudes
and
I am built this way to be
 be sold
away
into tar breast scraps

"You ain't no Queen"
Why, my legs aren't shaved on a hot day
My cooking is not your mother's'
My hair is nappy all of the time

When I smile, I'm not a whore
When I'm mad, I'm not an angry Black woman
My skin is out because my soul itches
The rules make me unapproachable
Body dipped in murky blue
Hand books
and
city landscapes
plagued across my lips
The messaging behind a lipstick shade
The message behind a pointed rifle
The message
expected to be there
and clear

like hurricane damage
upon a newborn black girl

Nikki

Nikki with Hakeem on her hip/looking for a dime /for a tip
You see she walking with her head high/ no time to regurgitate the
look in her eyes
She say she she's good /she don't need no help/gladly smiling with
a bulging baby bump feeling herself/She's like the supreme when
it comes to talking/when there is some kind of lending hand she
just keeps on walking

Nikki------

wishes for a secure blanket
where she won't be eaten

Where she won't have   too much pride
Yet he
continues to suck on shameless nipples   the smell of hot coal
underneath chin
and sometimes
the corner of her womanness begins to burst like seaweed and
wounded butterflies

Nikki so tough   she is all good/like chipped paint in water through
cracked wood/
You see her with a crooked smile/ramen noodles at Mr Chows/
Lifting up the streets with just a finger/her presence and piercing
bull mentality starts to linger/little Hakeem and baby number
two/have to understand the struggle, the pain, the truth

Nikki----

Doesn't know how to ask for hugs

Or an extra eye

Or a neckline

Or gauze

The leakage
Of God

Nikki---

Doesn't know how to find

chestnut hands

    that are big enough

to

  hug

neglected blood

Warning: This video contains graphic and disturbing material

BLOOD

When JESUS came
if you believe in him
he melted his wounds onto a man   or 3/5ths of him
he smelled of bullets and mustard   and picnic bamboo baskets

SHE

His girlfriend   the video   clouds clinging to the dashboard   her
initial response was that he had been shot in the arm   but devils in
bloodstream soaked seats

To be black while driving is to be dead while frolicking existence
on posters and hashtags

But she has that disease too   that's why his gun is still pointed at
her   her petty little mouth yapping off
and he knew
he was going to shoot him

"Please don't let my boyfriend be dead"

"Fuuuuuuuuuuuuuuuuuuuuuuuuck!"

Gun still pointed
she is supposed to do something else   entice me to shoot her   be
irrational like those other women   I'm used to
It could be

my word
against
that little girl
in the backseat

"It's okay mommy."

She will grow up quicker   despise authority
save pieces of blood from soaked leather
draw inferiority on her body like an underground tube
attend therapy sessions
Run red lights when no one is looking
Cram face into a black pillows
Speak to her mom in fragments
Smile only when asked to
Remember the sound of gunshots and shattered glass
Never ride in back seats
Trace her fist and never her hands

"It's okay mommy"

"Specifically how do I live free in this black body?"

-Ta-nehisi Coates

SHE

hears sirens blanketed over black lives matter shots

Sirens: alllllll brrrrrrrrrr allllll lives matter

"Do they mommy, do they?"
End of video.

Outside (black girl adventures)

My mother taught me to fly my own wound

let it heal in the skies where the oak

seduces the yellowish-pinkish fluid from knees

I would rub it like jelly on my lips

Push the flakes from my scab to make the beginning letter of my

name

crusted with pink mango

I rode my bike with sea on my shoulders

pulling me in to taste salt and flesh

on concrete cracks and little

Sallie Walker

 licking all

of the oil from bicycle chains

No knee pads

Just me, wind, and tongue

licking the cracks and blood

from the driveway

Parts of flesh, a tooth, and a strawberry creamsicle in hand

Black girl # 9 Winter Dance

My mama made me a rainbow
when she said I looked like nana

She put the yellow on my forehead
shining mixed with shea butter
and afro sweat

    Mama' I'm gone' to dance
Maybe twerk some
Maybe kiss some
Maybe wear the crown on my head
Let it tangle with my strands
Let it get stuck
So I can be queen all of the time

    I said in my head
My dress in Mississippi River
long and drowning in blue

She drove me
and I listened
to the hums of the road
the passing of flies against the windshield
My
legs
shook
when I stepped out

She kissed me goodbye
Said she'd be back

And there

he was
already dancing
moving the moon and my damp coils

And then I felt the pain in my feet
when my body trickled toward him
He gestured for me to dance

I moved with rigor
Yet sweet
Fell into myself
The bass filling my throat
with vibrations
that bled and seeped through lips
I wanted to say something I've been wanting to say
but time went by
and blood had hit the floor

He walked away
Stared at my alienness
danced with a girl who reminded me of gold leather
patented seats
Somewhere to park and stay in

Mama saw
What appeared to be
blood on my dress

I'm a woman now
I suppose
So I washed up
got dressed
Put on my mama's velvet lipstick
Danced with myself in the mirror

while mama sang something soulful
She told me that I had nana's hips

In that moment
it felt good to be home

Questions:

Can I touch your hair?   Can I rub your skin?

Can you twerk?

                    Were you born with a big booty?

Are you worthy?   Are you all the way Black?

Is that your real hair or nah?

Can we fuck?

Are you a bad bitch?

Do you sleep with the devil?

Do you believe in magic XXX (*wink*)

Do you think it's really rape if you enticed me with that dress?

Are you stuck up like the rest of them?

Do you smile often? Because you should.

Are you always this angry?

Did you audition for the bad girls club?

Do you have kids? Oh, do they have the same father?

Do you want me?

Do you want to feel wanted?

Can you throw away your voice and your color?

Can you just twerk? Please? Just twerk only. Just twerk. This hand justified. This. Don't speak.

Picnic

The rape was consensual
just like the orange was watermelon dressed up in red stained skirt

You saw her laugh
with the finger hooked in her mouth
gumbs like soul-less armies
swollen swarms of thumbs and fists

Each fruit fly
The corner of her thigh
The wings fluttering in an oiled cannon
with tops of heads
The checkered tablecloth with urine and suave lotion

She'd wait a while
place the watermelon seeds inside your urethra
make the sounds of gunfire
unprotected
no ducking for cover

a long while
the coat hanger wire
the fetus with eyes like marigolds
in summer

She's covered in red ink
a paper from school
a shoveled dent
along her shin

That skirt soiled with clustered folk
the kind of folk with songs about the negro

inside of their throats
You'd see her cradle placenta and strawberry
in a wrecking ship motion

Her skin tar and heavy
They tried to cover up the smell with
ginger pine
remnants from fresh clothes hanging

You saw her
just how'd you see the others
across the park in late afternoons
with lips like sulky flesh tubes

There was nothing more to do
but to bless the food

Black girl # 10 carefree

Because the world wants to cage her
Deprive her of wealth
Slut shame her knees
Monument her earthly breasts
then put them in rings

She

Stopped
caring
about your
two cents
lint
breath
shit
hands
That grip
at movable
shadows
along
coasts
rivers
In your waters
In your tears
In your fragility

She remembered not to shave

to not shake your hand   to remember yesterday   and move
in something

short and satin

               Petunia opening

Colorful
transitions
Ballet

     Towers

Beaches in thighs
Love in skin

She makes the impossible fold
She makes the world hold beauty

Parts of a _____

When did liberating the yoni become so powerful?

vagina concoction
 thinning of caved uterus   sweet labia and
dignified clitoris
trapped like
deep sea squids plummeting in
bellows of ocean

Ain't I a woman?

You are 14
not yet a woman
cocooning
into overdeveloped miniscule
sheets of flesh

You attend a pool party
"disturbance"
Police is called
You are wrestled to the ground
by a white male officer
No
he does not mistaken you for cattle

It's one in the same.

No damsel in distress
just weight placed on itsy bitsy bright colored bikini on you

A black girl
14

I'm sure he felt you squirm
your curves sinking into
slither
like a snake's meaderment
cushiony
a seat
on your back
wailing black limbs

nothing but meat

Aint I a woman?

not ever treated so delicately
thrown into jagged bleached wearing uniforms

Look at me
Look at my arm

You
and
Me
we are sisters
breast bold
brown
lines
our ancestors walking in puddles
with no jacket to cover

we just bathe in water

and pig's flesh
invading our bodies

for centuries
deep sea squid
creatures
between our legs

with ocean water
and
ships with many more of us
Sojourner and others

Truth be told
bikinis and handguns
one in the same

Say her name

They haven't released her name yet
her belly swollen with undeveloped life

27
black
female

More angst to pull the trigger

The thugette didn't listen
that's how she got shot

She probably got caught in a life full of crime
the color of her skin with eyes of satan
blanketed into a thick smoke
with brown wide noses
sniffing under her skirt

big mouth
maybe
The witness says there was this "back and forth"
SFPD

EXCESSIVE FORCE
FATAL

FAT
ABDOMEN   SLAVE   RUNAWAY   STOLEN VEHICLE
HIT   HIT   HIT

I wondered what her last breath was like
Maybe her breath was an invisible entity
Maybe she coughed up blood and tiny baby fingers
Maybe she crammed her fist into black steel
it's too late now
they haven't even released her name
May 19, 2016
Malcolm X Day

The Help

Be nice to everyone you meet

               Make peach cobbler

Be understanding

               Throw yourself over

Drink with us

               Engage with us

Nice lady

Peanut

Brittle

Make eye contact with everyone

Nice lady

Full duty

Tiresome extracted

Bliss

and stay blessed cards

We know that you're super

It's admirable

Walk on coals now

Bring us a slushie from 7-11

Is your hair real?

Can we pet your magical prowess?

Make me into a Beyonce dancing doll

Carry hot sauce in your bag at all times

just in case

we need it

Your fro is burning

Ignore

Stay hydrated and astute

Thanks for being completely understanding and approachable

You make it easier

On us all

I'd like to still touch your hair   even through flames

We enjoy

danger

and charisma

and you

being you

Black girl # 11 Harvard

13% of black folk

                    She makes yellow paint cringe

sunsets

Speak with tiptoed fabric around its windows

     Today,

She'd like to be invisible

Her daddy was #44

Her youth and

        stallion legs

photographed

---------Vantage point from back seats of rental cars with access to four cup holders

Filled with sweat of this one story

Of being seen and unseen at Harvard

Of her bestie being blonde and blue eyed

with uncontrollable laughter

like those times her bestie would see a movie

with abstract humor

and laugh until tomorrow

and it is accepted

because she can move and fill the space with shrills and valleys

--------- congratulations (other common black folk say)

Ivy League Black girl
Still magic

     Tomorrow she'd like to be seen

not on camera though

For who she is

really

Those

     plantain lilies

walking along lines

of inner elbow

and midnight

        She studies

We study

        They study

Her

Us

We

        Praise our reflection

Michonne

Darkest of darkest arms

Can't be loved
                        with a sword

tongue battered
                                with guarded follicles
with screams as loud as hounds
                                You can't feel

because you are tougher than nails in flesh
because you are inhuman and
those almond brown eyes can't be rummaged

Days slashing the undead
in
dark
tangy musk
in morning time

                        You're just like them

                covered in blood

walking past
smelling of grief
in black born clots

expressionless   and cat-eyed

you can't feel
because
 you manage   to hold it all in

Passing

One morning
when Donald Duck was sleeping,
I whispered to my childhood and remembered the way it was when
people would give me kisses and candies with rainbow swirls
the pretty one with red cheeks they'd called me

I'd hold hands with my auntie   walk to the corner store
buy lemonheads
and beef jerky
Folks would turn to see
her ashy ankles
my sunburned forehead
her nappy kitchen
my blue eyes
her big behind

Store Clerk: Yes, I'd like to report a kidnapping
There is a Black woman   real dark
 looks like the Mammy kind
yes
maybe she is baby-sitting the little girl
I'm sure   she's got a tight hold on her
She may be dangerous   uh huh yes
she certainly looks the part

Donald Duck was just about to say something that I could
understand
But in the moment he says
 oh boy oh boy oh boy   getting ready to greet Daisy

Auntie would make fun of me every time I'd eat a lemonhead
my lips puckering up

my eyes squinty
still enough light to see the baby blue

This is just routine   the policeman says

This is my niece   she says
Her hands firmly on her hips
me peeking around her waist side
What's the big deal?
Donald Duck would say usually
I'd turn off the T.V.
cover my eyes and
 trace my fingertips
run it along my skin
my blackness lost in translation somewhere

My lemonheads drop on the floor and he looks at me differently
Didn't even bother to help me pick them up or give me a smile

He knows now
He knows

Cake

Yesterday daddy came home.   He made a piñata.

I watched him. Filled her up with red. Bursted her open with jolly knuckles.

"Don't Eva talk back like your mother cus she got an ugly ghetto mouth on her."

She couldn't say "hey baby I'm alright this time."

This is what it looks like
with
my hands in gelato

      Hair and
skin
         On
mango taffy

      Red frosting
and
I couldn't eat cake this way
or ever

Mama,
Can you still speak?
Can you blow out the candles or even make a wish?

silence

Black girl #12 Rose

Picked off of the field
Severed in half by work boots
Opened to be silenced
Blushed on unwanted hands
Pricked
by
a bumble finger
The bruises lasting a lifetime

Twigs and Sun

He said
he would take me into the bathroom and shove it in me
all of his juice
I was confused
I was only 9
My dress
sun yellow
We've had days like this, the sun and I

His name Sun
My name unimportant
My skin in prepubescent sloth
His voice and many others like it
Forsaking branches with teeth
And me

*Girl's parents outraged after Texas school doesn't tell them boys
whipped and threatened to rape her*

WET TWIGS
Welts on my back

WET TWIGS
Welts on my back

They almost had me
Almost
My back burning

My dress burning
behind a bathroom stall.
Yellow
The stain of autumn
Smothering me

What I saw

My mother's tooth carved into maple wood

I grew up with images of men in clown masks with black hands

Maple wood
Sweet tooth

I always wanted to love his revolutionary power fist
His call for loving the black woman
His locs
The altar for burying deep thoughts and unyielding truths

Things we never spoke of aloud

After man number 4
Labia
fluctuating between an
 unrested bear
and
debris in the wind
Unfolding and imploding

He called me queen and let me go
Told me he had to leave his mark
Sniff me
Envelop me
Brush me with his black hands

He had the intensity of a lion
but the heart of a hyena
Pearls engulfed down his throat

Smile empress

Smile queen

Smile love
I was unseen

An attack on my worth

He had no capacity to love
To know
To really know
Just beyond the maple wood
Just beyond my mother's tooth
There
a little black girl
in broken pyramids

Black girl # 13 Momma

These hips born out of coasts and long winds

Because I had to change

Feed three emblems of myself

Yells echoed through the back of
my yawns

Nights
chile'
Nights
when I
give up on rest

I know

turning my back
like baba
would turn those children greener than

the backs of cheap earrings

How do you do it? They ask me.

I'd lose my life if I didn't.

"Naan Nigga" (Trick Daddy)

Momma pushed you out
you
your little toe hitting the ethers
hitting the cottony blood
doughy home
you'd swim
then cry black
from the bits and pieces of shard glass along
her legs

That shoe where my face hit
the putting of your mouth wear my fro lives
where my taste lives
where your mother once lived

Naan

Nope nope

You don't want no
pork and beans baby
Not today

She fed you though   she birthed you though   she
When you blame the coco fizzle through your nostrils
When you sucked those titties
When you saw that no man wanted your momma

Black.
Neglected.
The system was all she wrote
forced into her womb like bottle stoppers

to avoid the spoilage of taste.
Nobody wanted her

Nope. nope.

Scarred
with pork and beans running down her arms.
Dried snot stained on spoons.
Charred lips on tile floors.

The way you inhale blood from yesterday and
dance with your shirt off in Miami on the porch with a tired
wooden spoon.

An image of every black woman you see:

Maurice, you hungry
Maurice, nobody wants me
Maurice, It's pork and beans
Maurice, the blood clots won't stop

But it's useless
We are useless
like your momma
Naan nigga

Nope nope

The forgotten knots
The impact against her uterus

Today: amputated tongue willingly fed to those men who abused
your mother

Today: you smell her blood   the tiles   the comments the doctor
made in his mind

Another ghetto baby
In the hood

When you see me
your shoe plummets my face
think of her
washing your ass
but never the dried crack from your lips
She couldn't be there to do that, Maurice
Naan
Nope nope
Dirty
though the spite
left clean

You can have that Oxy

Oxy   on your lips from kissing sleeveless becky jenner   hannah
cassidy from a small town in Iowa called   Eldora

I knew it
I'd give you "tude" because I didn't like your opinions   I
decided to wear my go getter jumpsuit and sashayed around like
nobody's business   my body couldn't fit into Judy Jetson's
animated do as I say next century "we can live on mars and venus"
apparel.

Oxy and you miss
miss the cherry from these ethers and have decided to drop it in my
morning chamomile special cup

I knew it
Because my goals were travel   billion dollars and   extra
studies   I was neglectful like a mother to a newborn clinging
on to   breast that don't belong to her   that dry up and mourn
for youthful perky surgery gels and Dr. Weston or whatever his
name might be from Beverly Hills or some shit

Oxy
and you want the love that's neither hit nor miss   but fragile
co-dependent tragedies
and I'm not interested in squealing " I'm the man of the house"
parades

He then take his petty self in the booth like:
Take off that lipstick/ Who you tryna impress?
Business suit for what? /I work. You rest.
What,I just want you all to myself/ I must confess

But because of your attitude /I'm sticking with white girl /cuz there's no drama/ nor mess.

I knew it
Oxy on your finger tips   too much of ebony glaciers on the
calendar   too much of slaying and two snaps   like
Ella
Diana
Audre
Michelle
The golden brownie brown browns   the warmth of July in cities of
cocoa areolas
filled in the hips with 808 systems and
Billie Holiday frequencies from lips and simple breaths
Just like that

You hang to oxy
Go to Iowa
to be branded with bland

You still want that
Then so be it

Black girl # 14 Redbone girl

Because

the magenta in my face turns to devils   but some think
it's magical

I've tried charcoal

dark mahogany

tears from a girl 50 shades darker

to rub on my cheeks   yellow and chaotic

The kind of chaotic that leave the muscles to twitch involuntarily

Because people say I'm pretty

and fuckable because I'm bright   but that can be blinding

That can be

putting your face too close to sparklers and electric volts

That can be

dipping your fingers into mustard and sugar crystals

all to make a mess

But people say I'm pretty

They like my curls
and call me flower bud

They want to taste the devil who dances inside my cheeks
People say I'm not black enough

make me prove my lips are from Tunisia

But I can't and I won't

                  Sitting here to be pretty   picked from a tree
bitten and bloodied bone

Mars

mulatto gal from the south

the one that stays indoors

The one that makes the billboard

Gets put in a music video

              I didn't really make it   they don't
really like magic and devils dancing

I'll sit this one out

stand in the dark behind bushes

be in peace with the night sky   blues and blacks and twinkles of
me
spacious and unreachable   yellow

Scraped

The burnt parts
from toast

You've scraped
shoulders
which I've stood on
to see the real thing

No such thing

The burnt parts
from the tips you've burned

to secure the ends of my braids
but they've pulled it and
yanked my insides

The burnt parts
from my skin

two toned
aggressive sun
The line across my feet
The sandals
The part between toes
throbbing like Mars and unearthly times

The burnt parts
left alone
like my lips

They've turned away

all of them
They saw a woman like me
Brown
with a scalp so shiny
flaky crack oozing beyond the chair

The real cream

You've managed to seep through too many skulls
I've managed to get lost in those mazes and patterns imprinted on
burnt toast

All of those parts
All of them
You've scraped

Brunch with Badu

Tea leaves sit there   making its comeback in the air   we sip
and have herbs flying through our head wraps

Mama Badu
Can I ask you something?
What advice can you give me?
I'm trying sing with the breeze but   I think they have a problem
with my brownies   right there   the tips of my shoulders   the
definitions of those traps   muscles
Oh so you want milk with that?

You laugh when I twirl my hair and we talk about apple trees and
burning incense
We're friends
Those lyrics   and my pajamas   and cough syrup
I still try to sing and hum

passed me the sugar from your hips
HONEY
Pink finger
Green eyes
So much of me is you   you'd say

You told me you don't give out autographs
Just brunch and chats
You have significantly made this meal magic
from songs and palm rolls to twists
to afros and
knowing
the booty
don't lie
all love   Let's do this again soon

She

at the edge of the bed

spreading her jelly on spread

like

fragile poppies

glistening in shimmery tremors

sweet and brown

brown and

oiled

from sun shining in winter

and heater blasting

digging a grave from follicles

curling over

the abdomen

the

pocket holes of birth

the original afro

mama seeds

and black girl juice

She
steadily holding her knees to her stomach

with a long shirt

rocking with force of ten percussionists

swallowing and savoring the aroma

maple

city

between curves

of royalty

glute bridge

and permanency of painted coffee beans

penetrated deeply in skin

the radiant and unavoidable

shoulders

dripping

like candle wax

and ocean

She
shouldn't have to contemplate

or rub away the morning cups

filled to wake us all up
coffee bean

delight

rocking

where the winter sun

finds its' motivation

She

sweetly

inhaling

thunder thighs

and jelly

She

Woman

brown

orange

with cadence

of a thousand drums

She

She is

She be

light joy and

big breasted bird

with tides rolling on her lips

the rush of beauty

at the tips

She

God

and wondrous roars

from painted ruins

gold brown queen

at the end of bed

twisting coils

from her love patch

love

sweet saps and bloom

that is she

Black girl #15 Balance

Wearing Face

Insert picture here:
<tiny box braids and a "yass honey T-shirt">

Oh no wait wrong one:
<lace front>

No no no
<hair straightened

green eyes from father's side
half Indian/Persian
blue pant suit
boots with heel and diamond studded earrings
passed down from my great grandma Irene
the one with the natural blond hair
her mother's mother
German
my smile
just above your head
like marionettes dangling sweet brass monkey
slithering down throat
I

was just about to tell you

why I'm an independent strong black woman

but the waves just

<afro>

Wait….It was because my hair was wet

It was you that brought me here

<Egyptian musk>

Those were the beads my little sis gave me

I just keep them in a little jar of resistances

like my blue magic grease

even my bantu knots swirl around in there

like a dirty cocktail stirred and chilled

garnished with a cherry

<hide>

Only because my hands smell like black girl juice

because my anger is that of a gargoyle

at night

and my lips are the size of your thumb and index finger

curved around to form an O shape

Only because my skin

is not the forefront of that billboard down the street n

Only because my eyes aren't really green

Only because I own THOT dresses

<melanin>

I'd have to not be ashy today

I'd have to glow in the sun

like my momma and them do

The glory of faces

Foundation of my body

Balancing in a crooked room

<circus act>

REMY AND NICKI

aRe you DuMB

?

Pink cotton in the night
Sweat trap beats in the day
We've played this game with lip smackers gloss before
when were little girls
with our ring fingers wrapped with ring pops and yoyo strings

We've played around these yards
giving little boys the business with our bars
but this is different
Ma
Minaj

Ma minaj
hurts
where there are collages of earth straddling circumcisions
What's proper
diction
Men who are flattered with silicon and leopard pants prints

ARE YOU
DUMB

AM I THE ONE
WHO SHOT THE GUN

RUN SON MY SON YOUR SON
OUR WOMBS THE BROKEN CASE
FOR PAIN AND CONFUSION

So we beef
Plenty meat
Left out on the counter
Bodied
And
departed

Room for two
or one more
or
None

When it's over
there is the gun
the tear through lips
We've written through it
With ghostwriters staring like statues in all white
The blood from our tongues
covering silence
white rooms
blank pages
venom in nights
strobe lights and our fears of
post mortem pokes
Once we write
we shoot
then someone dies

We are gathered here today
We are
opportunists
and there is a chance to be revived
Ma minaj hurts
when we speak of surgeries and repairs

The lips in the night
The hand that picks them bloody smackers off of the floor
Pick it up
and shoot back

Mentality

Raised to argue
to defend scarred legs
that run from lions
while humming with sparrows
wanting to call my father a dad

Mornings
are of me scratching love off of my scalp
where edges bleed
Some mister would tell me that I'm just bitter
that I'm just a sour patch
a burnt orange on clouds

Raised to snap my fingers
demand accuracy
twist faces that doubt me
My mother said her womb was sometimes regretful
when I entered existence
It wasn't planned
so I'd shoot her looks to her throat

People stare
Say I have the damndest attitude
Born with that
argumentative wailing lip

That lip
and open thigh
That smoked gun
underneath my tongue
Raised hurt

Getting to know you getting to know all about you

My name
painted over tusks and Maya's bird cage
and
I was born clinging to my mother's nostril
in a time where Spring caused uproar
at noons and dawns

I
like long walks on the surface of danger
playing with
fire
and nights when
bands play behind my ears
with sounds of coconuts dropping
on lips and guitars
shifting its' riffs

I would like to imagine I have brothers and sisters
looking
like the shapes of women and men
in banned literature
in print ads in the 1900's
and sweet melanin
so deep with
purple and fall sky

I
am
afraid of being afraid
I am looking for friendship
with many

continents
with many
ozones
and
incomplete structures
My name
growing
wild bush
with djembe and
Tanzania whistles
They inhabit the sounds of maturity
felt in bones
and
in traditions susceptible to elephant tusks
and cages

Black girl #16 best friends

Took a long time to unthread me

Took a long time to bathe me

The fruits from unkempt baskets

The threading and pomegranate from my fingers

smeared like kindergarten painting on skin

        Because you tried to get my attention
Pull me closer

Play my husband even though you

put your woman against my unknown

You shouldn't have done that

You know

unleashing unicorns

with fixed eyes

Now my mother won't let me come home

Head Scarf

Show it!

Show me!

Hidden underneath is the down down down Mississippi river, lost notes, and old timer talks.

Up and down the curly foliage of braided black miss

Miss Mary black black black

hiding all of that that that

underneath that scarf scarf scarf

Three's a charm like french braids on picture days

The grief of an elbow

of a comb

struggling to make sense of the world

And where does it belong?

Where does all that strength come from?

Show it!

Show me and I'll show you mine!

Mine's

mixed with castles, thorns, and cotton fields

Those fields dare go past my shoulders

Tomorrow you'll wear the same purple scarf

with the blue magic grease stain

I know because I smell it

Smell you girl

Your mama said you can only play for a little bit

I can see just a bit of of the tail end of your braid

looking toward the sky

wanting to come down from the weight of the scarf

but it's a journey

so is mine

I know it

Know it all

underneath

Vile

It was

off with my cervix

    Traces of blood and benign fingers

like kids on International Blvd.   playing with rocks and silk
linens from curbsides

        He said   I was a sweet poppy

with lacerated tunnels

Plain ol' ring
Wear it around tongue
Wear it
Wear it like a mouth
        pressed against cold Atlantic cod

18
       Today was a birthday gift

The odor from his drawstring pants
I'd act like I didn't notice

Live with it
He'd say
before my internal shores were
taken over

and then poppy seeds
wouldn't harvest or return

I'd cut the rest of
the flaps in tide

On the couch

I asked if I could be a humming on your lap
where the knees form into congolese rumba sections

If I let my spit fall on the crotch of your denims
there would be sweet jazz folk song
tip toeing on dense murals

    You let me paint me
where thigh hairs
     become balconies with beads
from February

You say yes
sink into your magnolia
    My eyes open   but you don't know

I jam my waist into more buzz and afrobeat
    polyester fiber on the most sensational art

My body
the shape of harmony
All of the sound in my blood
All of the hums
All of the love

Black girl # 17 Love

Her
                    frizzy hair

against my nose

Seashells by the tone in her calling

like want

and

an army of horses

with her shoulders

               Fast

Smooth
                    Trails of happy fears

 her gaze

The offshore

The pillow

My chest

Her cheeks brown and hazelnut

I'm convinced of that power alone

A smile to keep a man full of lightning and instrumental jazz
Crackling

Striking

My lips in the present moment

moving with sundown

Im home.

Selection

We

Want

Her

*I was dressed in barnyard grass seeds welts and hand me down
vaginal fluid just from the last yellow girl she didn't say much
when she returned her mouth the color of cornmeal with just
a peck of granite on each knee

*He had mixture of uterine wall linings hanging off of him
dangling like rotten poultry that had been dried up in the sun
against a fence

The carpenter hasn't come in as of late ol' lumber still awaits
him with bits of crushed pepper and semen
He was a good negro carpenter Yet we all had to be reminded
of our times there

*She came back with hair filled with plantation dirt and
magnolia her youngest son was too wild though they had to
embed his wringing neck around her waist
Tar baby had to hug on to lady hips before they took the next one

We

Sang

and bled

fists and sugar

It's always the second time around that you bleed the most

*One of the pregnant girls' says she thinks about her unborn mutt
while her knees hug onto stench and grass   He said he could only
be gentle when she begins to enjoy it*

Having to wipe my face of urine and sage
I could still manage to smell the inner workings of the woman
before me and the woman before her and the woman before her
and the woman before her and the
sourness that penetrates over and over
Makes the bit of granite
sweet sounding

*He must like me   said the one in pigtails   I'm picked the
most*

Follow

Girl,

with projects on her fingernails

    around the way

Designs of roughnecks connecting to her keychain

    Home is westward

They follow

Come in a pack of cherry heads

    Soured talk

The way they look at your 7th wonder

saying things like,

"I want to unravel your world, cus I see it swaying in a hammock"

"I want to caress your shoulders and call them tree stalks
and I've practiced climbing with the
other 6 wonders"

You want to walk home in silence

There is noise in the ground
Newspaper
Boys
Girls

"Open"
You waver cuz you're dark purplish
Ink running like oil
You insert your world into a mechanic

filled with the Ganges river

and

herds

"Hold my hand, let me relax your body

near

dark shores

The tentacles are in my wallet

I'll pay for a time   Just jiggle your keys"

Oye como va
mi ritmo

My sister had keys jingling in her back pocket
an alarm clock for neighbors waiting to get on stoops to holler
I call her
Sheeba con lime
with flocks of herbs on her happy trail abdomen
and
fingertips
playing a
harp
downtown

Mi ritmo
is
keys jingling
legs swimming in pools
of coconut oil
and
hair
making love to
men's eyes
that stare
so deeply
at a woman with golden labels
on shoulders

Queen Sheeba con lime
I
saw her standing there
playing drums
with no hands

Grace comes from
honey tinted lips
with kinky sideburns
with purified brown skin
and passed down baskets
to put on our heads
to feed our children

My sister
walking
not to cause a scene
but to cause a stampede
elephant
necklaces
and rhino teeth
earrings
wild
natural
roots
from wombs
and sesame seeds
cultivated
in the irises of
Mothers

I
looking out a window
wondering where she walks
and how she uses her
glow
to captivate tiny
walks of life

I
mi ritmo
are locs
and
bangles
from
ancient
Egypt
on wrists

so I walk behind
my sister
and swallow a tiny
fragment from
her
skin
injera
cilantro
and lime

I wonder if I
could play drums
with no hands
or walk above the
grounds

If I could be one
like her
on a warm day
calling out
to the herds in Africa
calling out
to my people
oye como va

ella ritmo
y
mi ritmo
of Queens

Black girl # 18 Jasmine

Rubbed my lips pon' flower

The joy in lush   jelly in the
highlights of petals intermingling with honey songs

Rubbed my lips pon' zig zagged streets

Raced cars with my mind

Ran with

my fingers behind my aura

Hello
Yes
This is me

Is it real?

Yes

I grew up to be a small and subtle revelation scent

Jasmine

A revolution

A calm storm

A sweet but fiery creature
Not a doormat love
Love lives in spice, hair, afro blue genie, the ladies swinging along
coils, shimmery
shadow, the look on my daughter's face, approvals, the eyebrow,
the spit bubble love

Love

Is it real?

Rubbed my lips pon' blues and soul

Discovered a passage

        Called it wounded glamor

Small

but impactful

        Breath to keep the earth working

Breath pon' power

Pon' magic

        It's there

Magical bloom
        Don't underestimate

Bitter

Amber musk

   Swinging on my neck

Amber musk

   Where you left your tongue in

You

Planted yourself on mango seeds

Skin oceaned in dark horses

   You took rides
On
My
Back

   To carry your pretend self

A man
Or lack thereof
But this isn't really about you

When a Black woman with shipwrecked insides still loves
She carries moons
Troubles
Amber musk
Jasmine
Frankincense
Mandarin

Eucalyptus
Whatever scent you betrayed that day
Whatever scent you pretended to be to build
Whatever musk you sweated
Whatever musk you used to cover your illness
We want to find a rose mixed with lavender
Find your soul and smother it with chakra oil
Kiss your bones
With our wombs
Make you feel love
Make you feel love
Make you feel
Make you
Make
A
Mess
Is
What
You
Make
and then the next one
calls our mango bitter

*when you constantly fight for others and fight for others and fight
for others and fight for their demons and their dragon blood and
their unhappiness and their soul and their puke*

*we must fight for ourselves, for ethers, for our bodies, our hearts,
our souls, our selfcare, our magic, our wombs, our sanity, our
needs, our desires, our bitter, our sour, our hope, to allow ourselves
to be open once again*

Allergic to the word Woman

These hoes ain't loyal
But your momma is
And your sister
And your auntie is

**The first time my daddy called my momma a bitch
I was cleaning out my closet
I grabbed my head scarf and some Jergens lotion
retreated to the place behind the pink jelly bean stash
relaxed and drenched myself to become less ashy
Furthermore sweetening up my invisibility as a wo-

Wait we don't say that word
Hives are coming around this year
as well as summer dresses
Thots
with no panties on underneath
You
say you can lay your head
on that ass

**That day in class, Freshman year I was called a silly hoe
I grabbed my vulva
marked a red x
where only stitches enter
Walked out without anyone noticing

poof

Your Mother asks you about a particular dress she should got from
Ross
She doesn't know that you just saw two bad bitches with the
identical color
Spring lime
With the trim of the dress going diagonally

You hesitate
She says I think it's cute
"Ok momma, get it."

**That one time when I got on the bus coming back from school
these boys were talking about getting some girl number
"Oh she a thot bitch too"
"You can tell look at them duck lips."

------I held in my stitches as best as I could
yelled for my womb to appear fleshy and vibrant
but it cramped up into a miniscule hermit

Your mother wears that dress to a family picnic
The air is holding in words
People come and go
as the clouds jumble into an array of deep purple menstrual clots

** On my first date he told me that all of his previous girlfriends
were all bad bitches but they didn't know how to act.
My eyes watered
My breasts wandered off into a self detonated force field
I grabbed a handful of my juices   held on to the scent before I
wandered off entirely

At the picnic you ate your mama's mac and cheese
She tells you she needs your help
and then you hear it
You hear the rumbling a few feet away
The all too familiar
"Damn that bitch looks good"

You swallow a bit of the air
That's your momma
You tighten your fist
That's your momma
You forget about the bad bitches from last week
That's your momma
It's not the same
That's your momma

--The words silenced from the sky
and the only thing pouring
from the layout of the clouds
is woman
all on that picnic table
pollen
blood
and all of her invisibility

Headwraps

Avocado bandage

covering braids

the trickling of sweat   our mamas

shielding their earth from sun

Althea
Brenda
Pinky
The woman who blinks three times
when she wants to unwrap her soul
let her hair be intertwined with dirt and
cauliflower

Right there
They pray
Let them sing
Let them

Free BLACK WOMEN
with their ribbons
and patterns
and damaged roots atop their heads

Remember her
She tied a bow
With fabric from Nigeria

The color of lion growl

She had perfect teeth
hips that made the land unjust   the only way to make it right
was to have a seat
                    across the table with

Maya Angelou

Talk about the fabric of black women with high cheekbones and
thick noses

                    wrapped around her head

Freedom
Sojourner
And Lauryn Hill

        She said

We've begun to address the avocado wrap
mix it with mango and skylines from summer
mix it with sea and voices of our ancestors
Mix it with
black fists
purple nails
geometric equations from sunlight and red clay

Our headwrap

the colors of our voices
smooth
around our heads
in our minds forever

Black girl #20 Kenneka Jenkins (rest in peace)

help me

Music plays with me   and my reflection   plays tag with the
beast in you
with my spit in black pillows   with the comfort in queen sized
sheets and
liquor   plays with girls like me

help me

She was once my twin   my destruction   my see-saw   and I've
barely grown up to see the city light up with my heart exposed
my rope   my sad vocal   my version of an event of all of the
events

help

I may have trembled and swirled in vomit with you
and
laughed and shared a drink with you and passed and puffed
with her and I
BUT

me

You never wanted to know   but really wanted to know
when people fill up the room with paint
to see what your tongue looks like when it's green and blotchy
to smell the projects amongst walls from the ninth floor of a
hotel
to feel secure
with colors

and dancing brown ladies
and men with foam running down their chins

Find me here and there and clues that mislead   find your
friends with shades in the night
Find
Help
Find
me   (volume of music increases)

Math

I started off doing math on my belly

the squiggle lines just beyond the girdle

Math

and sometimes I'd dream of moons and painters with large
moustaches

calculating the areas of chin hairs and for colored only signs

I'd wait in line

keep my head down

Yes sir

Yes mam

The lines on my belly

telling me to stand up on those stars

make my brown pigment mix in with the galaxy

and those dreams

where the painter dedicates his work to his muse

Math

the equivalent to sharing sweat with a white woman

We'd be powdering our noses

Then I'd calculate how to send someone to the moon

Maybe me
Maybe we

I don't know

My head down

No sir no mam

That is not the right way you see....

then I'd go off into a black hole in their eyes

a place that they can't reach

but my kind can

I can

I can fly beyond those limitations

because of

Math

(hidden figures)

Black girl # 21 Raina (from Power)

She
dealt with roses

    the white ones that fall

        from daddy's breast pockets

where doves
pretended to be
plucked gardens
    leaking its blood to fit
inside
the
hour

    Laid down its' wing to be a treasure

    Baby girl
        in the realm of goodness and rot

because black girls are sacrificed in wings all of the time

    I would have told her:

reach and take the doves' spewing head
    Take the roses for yourself
    Don't wait for them to fall

because black girls are sacrificed in wings all of the time
like spring cleaning in blackberry fragrance
        We have to constantly give and let go

Black girl # 22 Me

11:11 am

To 2:22pm

The angel watching

me

put on face

I wear a brass section in my ribcage

A bird's nest

Its evolution

Inside throat

but

my back often hurts

and my neck hangs tilted

Mama told me

that I often try to take on the whole world

scoop up skeletons

scarf them down

cover the holes with sand castles

behave like unplanned migrations

Smiling with a cold steel against my tailbone

Mama,

I would say,

The world is too much for me sometimes

and the space swallows me without chewing

I am

every sister

mother's

daughter's

regurgitated lemon

soured in a summer dress in November

but when all is bright and magical

because those moments are star lights

        I am sweet lemon
in a tall glass with lavender

All my pain hails
The girls who look like me gather around the table

Discuss their potency

Make mine and their own skeletons full

        of flesh melanin and grapefruit

www.ingramcontent.com/pod-product-compliance
Lightning Source LLC
Chambersburg PA
CBHW051831090426
42736CB00011B/1751